AF228516

VOLODYMYR ZELENSKYY
PRESIDENT OF UKRAINE

BY CARLA MOONEY

Core Library

An Imprint of Abdo Publishing
abdobooks.com

Cover image: Volodymyr Zelenskyy became the face of Ukraine's
resistance after Russia's invasion.

abdobooks.com

Published by Abdo Publishing, a division of ABDO, PO Box 398166, Minneapolis, Minnesota 55439. Copyright © 2023 by Abdo Consulting Group, Inc. International copyrights reserved in all countries. No part of this book may be reproduced in any form without written permission from the publisher. Core Library™ is a trademark and logo of Abdo Publishing.

Printed in the United States of America, North Mankato, Minnesota.
052022
092022

Cover Photo: Ukrainian Presidency/Anadolu Agency/Getty Images
Interior Photos: Ukrainian Presidency/Anadolu Agency/Getty Images, 4–5, 10, 34–35, 40; Ronaldo Schemidt/AFP/Getty Images, 7, 45; Ukrainian Presidential Press Office/AP Images, 8, 43; Marianna Ianovska/Shutterstock Images, 12–13; Emilio Morenatti/AP Images, 15; Volodymyr Tarasov/Ukrinform/Future Publishing/Getty Images, 18–19; Vadim Ghirda/AP Images, 20; Sergei Supinsky/AFP/Getty Images, 22; Brendan Hoffman/Getty Images News/Getty Images, 23; Ludovic Marin/AFP/Getty Images, 26–27; Shutterstock Images, 31 (top), 31 (middle); Telnov Oleksii/Shutterstock Images, 31 (bottom); Anadolu Agency/Getty Images, 32; Red Line Editorial, 39

Editor: Alyssa Sorenson
Series Designer: Katharine Hale

Library of Congress Control Number: 2022936035

Publisher's Cataloging-in-Publication Data

Names: Mooney, Carla, author.
Title: Volodymyr Zelenskyy: president of Ukraine / by Carla Mooney
Other Title: president of Ukraine
Description: Minneapolis, Minnesota: Abdo Publishing, 2023 | Series: Newsmakers | Includes online resources and index.
Identifiers: ISBN 9781532199189 (lib. bdg.) | ISBN 9781098273194 (ebook)
Subjects: LCSH: Zelensky, Volodymyr, 1978---Juvenile literature. | Presidents--Biography—Juvenile literature. | Ukraine--Politics and government--Biography--Juvenile literature. | Government officials--Biography--Juvenile literature.
Classification: DDC 947.7086--dc23

CONTENTS

CHAPTER ONE
Inspiring Ukraine and the World 4

CHAPTER TWO
Entertaining Early Years 12

CHAPTER THREE
Jumping into Politics 18

CHAPTER FOUR
President Zelenskyy 26

CHAPTER FIVE
A Wartime Leader 34

Important Dates 42

Stop and Think 44

Glossary 46

Online Resources 47

Learn More 47

Index 48

About the Author 48

INSPIRING UKRAINE AND THE WORLD

On the morning of February 24, 2022, sirens sounded around Kyiv, the capital of Ukraine. Explosions blasted across the country. Rocket attacks and shelling hit some big cities. Russian tanks and troops came over the border into Ukraine. The Russian invasion of Ukraine had begun.

Minutes before the attacks, Russian president Vladimir Putin said he planned to take away Ukraine's military power. People around the world were shocked. It was the

In 2022, Ukrainian president Volodymyr Zelenskyy visited troops to help boost morale.

UKRAINIAN INDEPENDENCE

For decades, Ukraine was one of the republics, along with Russia, that made up the Soviet Union. In the early 1990s, the Soviet Union began to fall apart. In 1991, Ukraine declared its independence. At the time, 92 percent of Ukrainian voters wanted this. Other former Soviet republics also became independent countries, including Belarus and Georgia.

biggest military action in Europe in many years.

THREAT OF WAR

Hours earlier, Ukraine's president, Volodymyr Zelenskyy, went on television. He spoke to the 44 million people in Ukraine as the threat of war grew. Then he asked the people of Russia to stop their leaders from sending troops into Ukraine. In his emotional message, he talked about the close ties between the people of Russia and Ukraine. Speaking in Russian, Zelenskyy asked for peace. He also warned that Ukraine would defend itself against a Russian invasion. "We know for sure we do not need a war," he said. "But if these forces

attack us, if you attempt to take away our country, our freedom, our lives, the lives of our children, we will defend ourselves."

Russian forces attacked Ukraine. Zelenskyy rallied his troops and people. He declared martial law. He also signed an order to prepare Ukraine's military forces and get supplies for war. Zelenskyy was in great danger, but he refused to leave his people. The United States said it could get him out of Kyiv. Zelenskyy turned down the offer. "The fight is here; I need ammunition, not a ride," he told US officials.

Throughout the invasion's first day, Russian missiles rained down on Kyiv. Russian troops wanted to cut off the capital from western Ukraine. The Russians had already captured areas north of the city. Yet the Ukrainians held Kyiv. Zelenskyy's government passed out 70,000 AK-47 rifles to citizens. Radio stations gave instructions on how to make handmade bombs. The city readied itself for the possibility of street fighting with Russian troops.

Zelenskyy appeared in a simple but powerful video message on February 25. That night, he stood in front of the presidential building in Kyiv. He wore military green. His top advisers stood with him.

His message to the Ukrainian people and the world was simple. "We are here. We are in Kyiv. We are protecting Ukraine," he said.

FROM COMEDIAN TO WARTIME LEADER

Zelenskyy had become a wartime leader in a few short days. Years before, he was working as a television actor and comedian. At that time, Zelenskyy had no real government experience. He had only played a president on television. Even so, he ran for president in 2019. He won in a landslide. But some people weren't sure about Zelenskyy's ability

REFUGEE CRISIS

Russia's invasion of Ukraine started a refugee crisis. People fled their homes to escape the violence. Millions of people moved to other parts of Ukraine or left the country. Neighboring countries gave them food, medical care, and basic supplies. They also helped refugees find housing and jobs. As his people suffered, Zelenskyy asked for peace talks with Russia to end the conflict.

to lead. Many of the advisers he picked also had little experience in government. None had experience leading a country in wartime.

Nevertheless, in February 2022, Zelenskyy rose to the moment. As a wartime leader, he united his country. He motivated citizens to fight. Zelenskyy also inspired the world. He made impassioned speeches to leaders around the globe. This led to a flow of foreign supplies and aid to Ukraine. There were many photos taken of Zelenskyy in the streets of Ukraine's war-ravaged cities, comforting his people. Zelenskyy's actions made him a hero at home and abroad.

STRAIGHT TO THE
SOURCE

President Zelenskyy spoke to members of the US Congress on March 16, 2022:

Today it's not enough to be the leader of the nation. Today . . . to be the leader of the world . . . means to be the leader of peace. Peace in your country doesn't depend anymore only on you and your people. It depends on those next to you and those who are strong. Strong doesn't mean big. Strong is brave and ready to fight for the [lives] of his citizens and citizens of the world. For human rights, for freedom, for the right to live decently, and to die when your time comes, and not when it's wanted by someone else, by your neighbor.

Source: Catie Edmonson. "Annotated Transcript: Zelensky's Speech to Congress." *New York Times*, 16 Mar. 2022, nytimes.com. Accessed 26 Apr. 2022.

WHAT'S THE BIG IDEA?

Read this portion of Zelenskyy's speech carefully. What is the main idea in the speech? Which details support the main idea? Name two or three details Zelenskyy uses to support his main idea.

ENTERTAINING EARLY YEARS

Volodymyr Zelenskyy was born on January 25, 1978. He was part of a working-class Jewish family. They lived in Kryvyi Rih. This is a city in southern Ukraine. Volodymyr's father was a mathematician. His mother was an engineer. Like others who lived in the area, Volodymyr grew up speaking Russian. He also spoke Ukrainian and English. During his childhood, Ukraine was part of the Soviet Union. Ukraine became independent in the early 1990s.

Kryvyi Rih has iron-ore deposits. It is an important mining city.

ENTERTAINING AUDIENCES

Volodymyr liked theater. At age 17, he joined a comedy group with his friends. The group was named Kvartal 95 after the neighborhood where they had lived. Kvartal 95 performed around Ukraine and eventually in Russia. In 1997, Kvartal 95 was in the finals of KVN. This was a popular comedy competition. It was broadcast on television. Volodymyr and Kvartal 95 appeared regularly on KVN for several years. They gained fame in Ukraine for their comedy skits.

Zelenskyy performed with Kvartal 95 for a long time. He grew comfortable in front of large audiences and cameras.

As a young man, Zelenskyy also studied at the Kyiv National Economic University. He graduated with a law degree in 2000. After his law school graduation, Zelenskyy entered the entertainment business full time. In 2003, he cofounded Studio Kvartal 95. This was a production company. It became one of the most successful entertainment studios in Ukraine. For many years, Zelenskyy worked as the company's artistic director. He appeared in several of the company's films. He often played the starring roles in romantic comedies. In 2006, Zelenskyy appeared in and won the Ukrainian version of the television show *Dancing with the Stars*.

RUSSIAN AGGRESSION AND
A HIT TELEVISION SITCOM

Zelenskyy was working on a television show when Ukraine was dealing with political unrest. In February 2014, Ukrainian president Viktor Yanukovych was removed from office. There had been months of protests against his government. In May 2014, billionaire Petro Poroshenko was elected to replace him.

Russia was upset at the changes. The Russians had supported Yanukovych. His removal meant Russia did not have as much influence in Ukraine. Soon after Yanukovych left office, Russia invaded and annexed Crimea. This is a Ukrainian region just south of the country. Rebels supported by Russia began to take areas in eastern Ukraine too. They wanted these areas to be under Russian control. Fighting between Ukraine's military and the rebels broke out.

It was in this environment in 2015 that Zelenskyy's biggest hit, a television sitcom called *Servant of the People*, first aired. In the show, Zelenskyy played the role of a high school history teacher. In one episode, the teacher rants against government corruption. A student films the teacher's rant and posts it on YouTube. Then the video goes viral. It captures people's attention right before a presidential election. The voters pick the history teacher to become the country's next president. The show and its main character's path to the presidency entertained millions of fans.

Zelenskyy is married to Olena Zelenska. She is a professional comedy writer. The couple met while in school. They got married in 2003. They have two children. As the First Lady of Ukraine, Zelenska has stood by issues such as women's safety, children's health, and disability access. When the Russians invaded Ukraine in 2022, Zelenska and her children remained in the country despite the risks to their safety.

JUMPING INTO POLITICS

n 2018, Ukrainian president Petro Poroshenko faced criticism. There were some people who said that he put business interests before the country. Others said his government was corrupt. Even worse, pro-Russian rebels continued to cause problems in eastern Ukraine. Many people were not happy about that. At the same time, the economy had stalled. Increasing prices hurt many citizens. As a result, Poroshenko's approval ratings sank very low.

Petro Poroshenko's unpopularity with the Ukrainian people caused many of them to dislike established politicians.

ELECTION CHALLENGERS

Poroshenko's low ratings opened the door to political

challengers. More than three dozen candidates entered

the 2019 presidential race. One of those candidates was

Volodymyr Zelenskyy.

At the time, Zelenskyy had no political experience.

But he wanted to help Ukraine. In 2018, Kvartal 95

officially registered Servant of the People as a political party. On New Year's Eve in 2018, Zelenskyy posted a video on YouTube. In the video, he stood next to a Christmas tree. Zelenskyy said that he was running for president.

ZELENSKYY'S CAMPAIGN

Zelenskyy's entry into the presidential race surprised many politicians. He was a comedian with no experience in government. People wondered how he could lead a country. Zelenskyy did not campaign in a traditional way.

A NEW POLITICAL PARTY

In 2018, Servant of the People became a political party in Ukraine. The party was named after the hit Ukrainian television sitcom. The party is primarily centrist in its policies. It has attracted a wide range of people because of its inclusiveness. It serves as a balance to the pro-western European Solidarity party and the pro-Russian Opposition Platform for Life party. Zelenskyy is a member of the Servant of the People party.

Instead, he traveled with his comedy group. Their show made fun of politicians and had humorous acts. In Kyiv, the city's largest concert hall sold out tickets to the show.

Zelenskyy promised to clean up the corruption in Ukrainian politics. Voters who were unhappy with the country's path flocked to him. As a native Russian speaker, Zelenskyy also won over millions of Russian-speaking Ukrainians living in the south and east. Many of these people had felt left behind by previous governments.

Zelenskyy's charm and anti-corruption messages
energized his supporters. Meanwhile, his critics doubted
the comedian could be a leader. They did not believe
he would be able to stand up to Russian president
Vladimir Putin. They feared Ukraine would fall under
Russia's control.

THE 2019 ELECTION

On March 31, 2019, Ukrainians went to the polls.
In Ukraine, people directly elect the president. The
winning candidate needs at least 50 percent of the
vote. If no one reaches 50 percent, the top two people
advance to a second election. In the first election,
Zelenskyy won more than 30 percent of the vote. In the

Zelenskyy celebrates after it was projected he won the Ukrainian presidency.

second election against Poroshenko, Zelenskyy won in a landslide. More than 73 percent of voters chose him.

Zelenskyy became president on May 20, 2019. In his first speech as president, he announced the breakup of Ukraine's parliament. The move triggered snap elections for parliament seats in July 2019. This action allowed Zelenskyy's political party to win a majority of seats in the parliament. For the first time in Ukraine's history, a single political party could control the legislature's agenda.

STRAIGHT TO THE
SOURCE

After Zelenskyy won Ukraine's presidential election in 2019, Jonah Fisher, a political analyst with BBC News, wrote this assessment:

The pressure will now be on Mr. [Zelenskyy] to demonstrate that he knows what he is doing. Throughout the election campaign, he avoided serious interviews and discussions about policy—preferring instead to post light-hearted videos to social media. He's got about a month before the inauguration. Then the comedian-turned-president will be faced with a complex in-tray that includes a simmering war with Russian-backed rebels in the east.

Source: "Ukraine Election: Comedian Zelensky Wins Presidency by Landslide." *BBC*, 22 Apr. 2019, bbc.com. Accessed 26 Apr. 2022.

CHANGING MINDS

This text passage questions whether Zelenskyy is prepared to be the president of Ukraine. Imagine you voted for Zelenskyy. How would you make your case in support of him? Make sure you explain your opinion. Include facts and details that support your reasons.

PRESIDENT ZELENSKYY

One of Zelenskyy's main campaign promises was to end the fighting in eastern Ukraine. Ukraine and Russia share a long border. At the time, the Ukrainian military and Russian-backed rebels battled in the Donbas region of eastern Ukraine. Both Russia and Ukraine believed this area was rightfully theirs.

In December 2019, Zelenskyy met with Russia's president, Vladimir Putin, in Paris, France. It was the first face-to-face

Zelenskyy shakes hands with French president Emmanuel Macron after arriving in Paris in 2019.

NATO

The North Atlantic Treaty Organization (NATO) is a multinational security alliance. That means multiple countries work together to promote peace and defend each other if attacked. It was created in 1949. When the Soviet Union fell in 1991, NATO expanded to include many new countries. Some of these included old Soviet republics. In 2008, the organization said it planned to have Ukraine join the alliance one day. Russia believes NATO's powerful military alliance is a threat to Russia's security. In early 2022, NATO had 30 member countries.

meeting between the two leaders. They discussed ways to end the fighting, but they could not find a compromise. Ukraine wanted to restore its control of the Donbas region. Russia wanted Ukraine to grant more control to the Donbas regional government, which was led by pro-Russian leaders.

Russia also wanted to prevent Ukraine from building stronger ties with Western countries. Russia wanted to stop Ukraine from joining the European Union. This is a political and economic group made up of

European countries. Russia also didn't want Ukraine to join the North Atlantic Treaty Organization (NATO). Meanwhile, Russia sent more money, equipment, and fighters to eastern Ukraine.

FROZEN AID

In the summer of 2019, the US government froze $400 million in military aid for Ukraine. The United States was an important Ukrainian ally. The aid was meant to help the Ukrainian military. The freeze was part of the Trump administration's effort to cut down on foreign aid. However, some people questioned whether it was meant to put pressure on Zelenskyy to investigate corruption claims against Donald Trump's political rival Joe Biden.

Zelenksyy did not look into any claims of corruption. The Trump administration eventually reinstated the vital military aid to Ukraine. Even so, some people believed that the issue weakened Ukraine's efforts in preventing Russian aggression.

ZELENSKYY AND COVID-19

In late 2020, scientists made vaccines for COVID-19. The vaccines helped prevent hospitalization and death. Zelenskyy urged Ukrainians to get vaccinated. He got vaccinated to show people the vaccine was safe and effective. However, Ukrainians were slow to get the vaccine or did not think they needed it. Some doubted the virus was as bad as people said. Many people did not trust the government or the vaccine. As a result, Ukraine had one of the lowest vaccination rates in Europe.

A PANDEMIC STRIKES

In 2020, the COVID-19 pandemic swept around the world. Many people caught the disease and got sick. Some people's cases were serious, and they died.

President Zelenskyy and his advisers created a plan. They wanted to limit the spread of the deadly virus. The plan included lockdown measures and business closures. However, enforcement of these things was difficult. Many people did not like the lockdown. Businesses and other groups protested.

COVID-19 IN UKRAINE

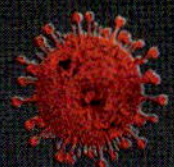

More than five million people in Ukraine got COVID-19.

More than 108,000 people in Ukraine died from COVID-19.

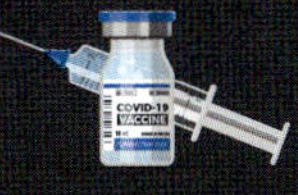

By May 2022, only 35.7% of the Ukrainian population was fully vaccinated.

During the pandemic, nations tried to keep COVID-19 from spreading. Still, many people got sick and died from the disease. How does the graphic help you understand how Ukraine was impacted by COVID-19?

Some businesses ignored the rules. They operated as they wished. Police were accused of taking bribes from businesses to not report rule breakers.

DECLINING TRUST

Ukraine had struggled with corruption in government and business for years. Zelenskyy said he would put an end to it. But once in office, some people believed he did not do enough.

A year into his presidency, public trust in Zelenskyy's government declined. He had delivered on few of his election promises. Fighting in eastern Ukraine continued. His approval rating was going down.

A NEW THREAT

In late 2021, Russia began a buildup of troops and equipment along its border with Ukraine. More Russian forces moved into neighboring Belarus, a Russian ally. Western officials warned that these movements showed Russia intended to invade Ukraine. Putin denied this. But Russia continued to prepare its military.

At first, Zelenskyy tried to downplay the threat of a Russian invasion. He told his people not to panic. By February 2022, however, war was increasingly likely. On February 21, 2022, Putin said that Russia would recognize Ukraine's Donbas region as independent. Three days later, on February 24, he announced a special military operation to free the area. Now President Zelenskyy faced the most serious threat of his presidency: war.

EXPLORE ONLINE

Chapter Four discusses Ukraine's history of conflict with Russia. The website below further explores this conflict. As you know, every source is different. What facts does the website give about the Ukraine–Russia conflict? How is the information from the website the same as the information in Chapter Four? What new information did you learn from the website?

RUSSIA'S AT WAR WITH UKRAINE. HERE'S HOW WE GOT HERE

abdocorelibrary.com/volodymyr-zelenskyy

A WARTIME LEADER

Russian forces invaded Ukraine in February 2022. Europe faced a ground war. It reminded many people of the early days of World War II (1939–1945). As the tanks rolled and bombs fell, President Zelenskyy delivered wartime messages to the people. In this time of crisis, Zelenskyy stood firm in his defense of Ukraine. He used his voice and ease in front of a camera to spread messages that inspired his country and the world.

Throughout the conflict, Zelenskyy supported and encouraged Ukrainian troops.

RUSSIANS ADVANCE

Russian forces poured into Ukraine. Their goal was to overrun Ukraine and replace its government. Russia wanted to end Ukraine's ambition to join NATO. Russia also wanted more control over Ukraine's government.

In the war's early days, Russian forces bombed several Ukrainian cities. They targeted cities such as Kharkiv in the east and Mariupol in the southeast. They attacked Kyiv in central Ukraine too. Russians also captured the inactive Chernobyl nuclear power plant in northern Ukraine.

ASSASSINATION ATTEMPTS

Since the beginning of the war, President Zelenskyy claimed that he was Russia's number one target. According to reports, he survived multiple assassination plots. A few of the plots failed after Russians against the war warned the Ukrainians about military groups planning to assassinate the president. Zelenskyy also said that Russian assassins targeted his wife and children.

Within days, Russian forces were focusing their attacks on Kyiv. By March 1, a 40-mile (64-km) convoy of Russian tanks and troops moved toward the capital city. Putin and the Russian forces expected to win quickly. They had more weapons and troops than the Ukrainians. They also believed the Ukrainians would not put up much of a fight.

FIERCE RESISTANCE

However, the Russians had underestimated the will of Zelenskyy and the Ukrainian people. Fierce resistance slowed Russian forces. Difficulty moving necessary supplies also slowed the Russian troops. Despite repeated attacks, the Ukrainians held Kyiv. They used weapons supplied to them by Western countries.

The Russians were unable to take the capital city. They were forced to change their plan. By late March, Russia shifted troops away from Kyiv. It was a surprising defeat for the Russian military. However, Russia continued fighting for other areas in Ukraine.

RALLYING THE COUNTRY AND ITS ALLIES

As the war started, Zelenskyy's experience in theater and television became a powerful tool. Seemingly overnight, he became the face of Ukrainian resistance. He used his smartphone and social media to talk with his people and the world. When the Russians claimed he had fled Kyiv, Zelenskyy filmed himself standing on the city streets. When the Russians said that neo-Nazis in Ukraine were using children as human shields, Zelenskyy responded with social media posts that showed otherwise. With each message, the people were reassured. Many Ukrainians were energized by their president's familiar face and earnest voice.

Zelenskyy's messages quickly spread beyond Ukraine's borders. He delivered emotional video addresses to leaders and governments worldwide. He urged nations to send military aid to Ukraine. He also pressed countries to limit Russia's ability to attack Ukraine in any way possible. Zelenskyy also tried to

RUSSIAN FORCES IN
UKRAINE

The situation in Ukraine was constantly changing. Russia's original goal was to take over Ukraine and its government. When this failed, Russia focused its efforts on taking Ukraine's southern and eastern regions. By July 2022, Russia had control of some of these areas. How does the map help you understand the conflict in Ukraine?

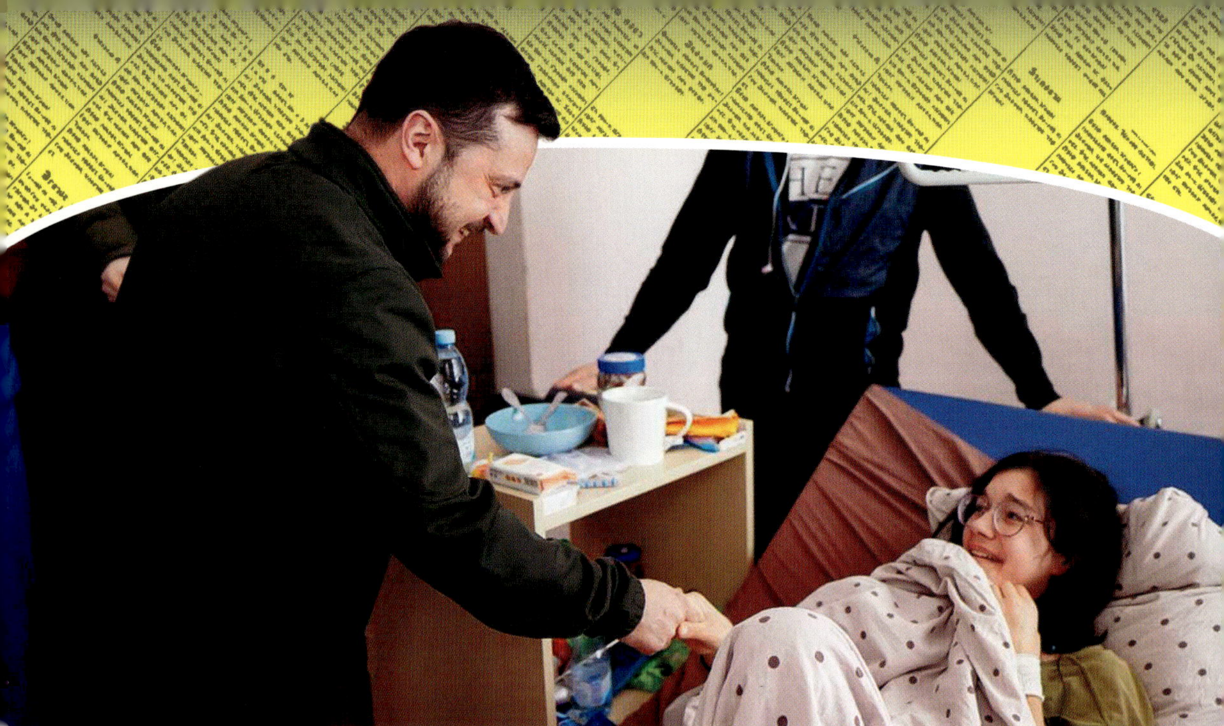

In March 2022, Zelenskyy visited a Kyiv hospital to see patients who had been hurt during the Russian invasion.

convince NATO countries to enforce a no-fly zone over Ukraine to stop Russian air raids.

Zelenskyy's personal appeals to the world community were mostly successful. Western countries, including the United States, sent weapons and other critical supplies to the Ukrainian military. They announced harsh economic sanctions on Russia. The Russian economy suffered significantly as a result. However, NATO chose not to enforce a no-fly zone over Ukraine. To do so, it might have to shoot down

Russian planes. Such an action would be considered an act of war against Russia. It would drag other countries directly into the conflict.

As the war progressed, Zelenskyy continued to stand by his country and people. He kept fighting for them. He tried to get as much international support as possible. Throughout the chaos, Zelenskyy continually called on Russia and the world to find a way toward unity and peace.

FURTHER EVIDENCE

There is a lot of information about Zelenskyy as a wartime leader in Chapter Five. If you could pick out the main point of the chapter, what would it be? Find a few pieces of key evidence from the chapter that support the main point. Then explore the website below to learn more about Zelenskyy. Find a quote from the website. Does the quote support an existing piece of evidence in the chapter? Or does it add a new piece of evidence?

FROM COMEDIAN TO WARTIME LEADER

abdocorelibrary.com/volodymyr-zelenskyy

IMPORTANT DATES

1978
On January 25, Volodymyr Zelenskyy is born in southern Ukraine.

1991
The Soviet Union falls apart. Several former Soviet republics, including Ukraine and Russia, become independent countries.

2003
Zelenskyy marries Olena Zelenska.

2015
The television sitcom *Servant of the People*, starring Zelenskyy, airs. It becomes a massive hit in Ukraine.

2019
Zelenskyy wins Ukraine's presidential election by a landslide with more than 73 percent of the vote. Later that year, the US government temporarily halts military aid to Ukraine.

2020
The COVID-19 pandemic strikes Ukraine and the world.

2022
On February 24, Russia launches an invasion of Ukraine. It begins with rocket attacks and shelling that strike several major cities.

February–March 2022
Zelenskyy appeals to world leaders to help Ukraine repel the Russian invasion. Many countries respond by sending military aid to Ukraine and issuing severe economic sanctions against Russia.

Tell the Tale

Chapter Five of this book discusses how Zelenskyy used his background as an entertainer to help him as a wartime leader. Imagine you are leading a country during a war. Write 200 words about what you would do to help your country and its citizens. How would you get your message out to the world?

Surprise Me

Chapter Two discusses Zelenskyy's life before politics. After reading this book, what two or three facts about his early life did you find most surprising? Write a few sentences about each fact. Why did you find each fact surprising?

Dig Deeper

After reading this book, what questions do you still have about Zelenskyy? With an adult's help, find a few reliable sources that can help you answer your questions. Write a paragraph about what you learned.

Say What?

Studying Zelenskyy and Ukraine can mean learning a lot of new vocabulary. Find five words in this book you've never heard before. Use a dictionary to find out what they mean. Then write the meanings in your own words and use each word in a new sentence.

GLOSSARY

annex
to add territory by force

corruption
dishonest behavior by people in power

economy
a system in which services and goods are made, bought, and sold within a country

martial law
law used by military forces during an emergency when public safety and order are at risk

neo-Nazi
someone who supports the policies of the Nazi Party, which controlled Germany from the 1930s through World War II

no-fly zone
a designated area over which aircraft may not fly, especially during a conflict

parliament
a type of legislative body

viral
describing an image or video on the internet that spreads rapidly

ONLINE RESOURCES

To learn more about Volodymyr Zelenskyy and Ukraine, visit our free resource websites below.

Visit **abdocorelibrary.com** or scan this QR code for free Common Core resources for teachers and students, including vetted activities, multimedia, and booklinks, for deeper subject comprehension.

Visit **abdobooklinks.com** or scan this QR code for free additional online weblinks for further learning. These links are routinely monitored and updated to provide the most current information available.

LEARN MORE

Gieseke, Tyler. *NATO*. Abdo, 2023.

Hopkinson, Deborah. *Where Is the Kremlin?* Penguin, 2019.

Wheeler, Jill C. *Volodymyr Zelenskyy*. Abdo, 2023.

INDEX

Belarus, 6, 32, 39

comedian, 9, 14–15, 17, 21–23, 25
COVID-19, 30–31

Donbas region, 27–28, 33

election, 9, 17, 23–25, 32

Judaism, 13–14

Kvartal 95, 14–15, 20
Kyiv, 5, 7–9, 22, 36–39

martial law, 7
military aid, 29, 38
missiles, 8

Nazis, 14, 38
North Atlantic Treaty Organization (NATO), 28–29, 36, 40

Poroshenko, Petro, 16, 19–20, 24
Putin, Vladimir, 5, 23, 27–28, 32–33, 37

rebels, 16, 19, 25, 27
refugees, 9
Russia, 5–9, 14, 16–17, 19, 21–23, 25, 27–29, 32–33, 36–41

Servant of the People, 16–17
snap elections, 24
Soviet Union, 6, 13–14, 28

Trump, Donald, 29

Yanukovych, Viktor, 16

Zelenska, Olena, 17, 36

About the Author

Carla Mooney is a graduate of the University of Pennsylvania with a degree in economics. Today, she writes for young people and is the author of many books for young adults and children.